Welcome to the Library

By Alyse Sweeney

Sydney
g

These content vocabulary word builders are for grades 1–2.
Subject Consultant: Carl A. Harvey II, Library Media Specialist,
North Elementary School, Noblesville, Indiana

Reading Consultant: Cecilia Minden-Cupp, PhD, Former Director of the Language and
Literacy Program, Harvard Graduate School of Education, Cambridge, Massachusetts

Photographs © 2007: Alamy Images: 5 bottom left, 13 (Phillip Little/Horizon International
Images Limited), 5 top left, 11 (Ed Young/AGStockUSA, Inc.); Corbis Images: 5 bottom right, 15
(Steve Chenn), 23 bottom left (Erik P./zefa), 23 top left (Royalty-Free), 23 top right (Joseph Sohm/
ChromoSohm Inc.); Getty Images: 21 top left (George Doyle & Ciaran Griffin), back cover, 2, 19
(Bruce Laurance/The Image Bank); James Levin Studios: 4 top, 5 top right, 10, 17, 21 bottom;
JupiterImages/Comstock: 1, 4 bottom left, 7; Monty Stilson: 4 bottom right, 12, 20, 21 top right;
PhotoEdit/Spencer Grant: 9; photolibrary.com/Digital Vision: cover; SODA/IPG: 23 bottom right.

Book Design: Simonsays Design!
Book Production: The Design Lab

Library of Congress Cataloging-in-Publication Data

Sweeney, Alyse.
  Welcome to the library / by Alyse Sweeney.
    p. cm. — (Scholastic news nonfiction readers)
  Includes bibliographical references and index.
  ISBN-10: 0-531-16841-7
  ISBN-13: 978-0-531-16841-7
  1. Libraries—Juvenile literature. 2. Librarians—Juvenile
literature. I. Title. II. Series.
  Z665.5S94 2007
  027—dc22   2006015655

1 2 3 4 5 6 7 8 9 10 R 16 15 14 13 12 11 10 09 08 07

CONTENTS

WORD HUNT

Look for these words as you read. They will be in **bold**.

call number
(**kawl nuhm**-bur)

librarian
(lye-**brer**-ee-uhn)

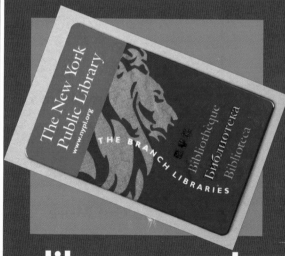

library card
(**lye**-brer-ee **card**)

computer
(kuhm-**pyoo**-tur)

display
(diss-**play**)

scanner
(**skan**-uhr)

story hour
(**stor**-ee **our**)

A Place to Find Answers

Who lives in a swamp?

Why do stars shine?

Visit the library and ask a **librarian**.

A librarian will help you find the answers to all your questions!

Librarians enjoy showing people how fun it is to read.

A librarian has many jobs.

One job is to buy all the books.

But you won't just find books at a library! Librarians also buy CDs, DVDs, magazines, and newspapers for the library.

This librarian puts videos on a shelf.

The librarian gives each new item a **call number**.

The call number is typed into the **computer**.

call number

People use computers to find different items in the library.

Librarians are great at helping you find just what you need.

And with a **library card**, you can take items home!

This library worker uses a **scanner** to keep track of items leaving the library.

library card

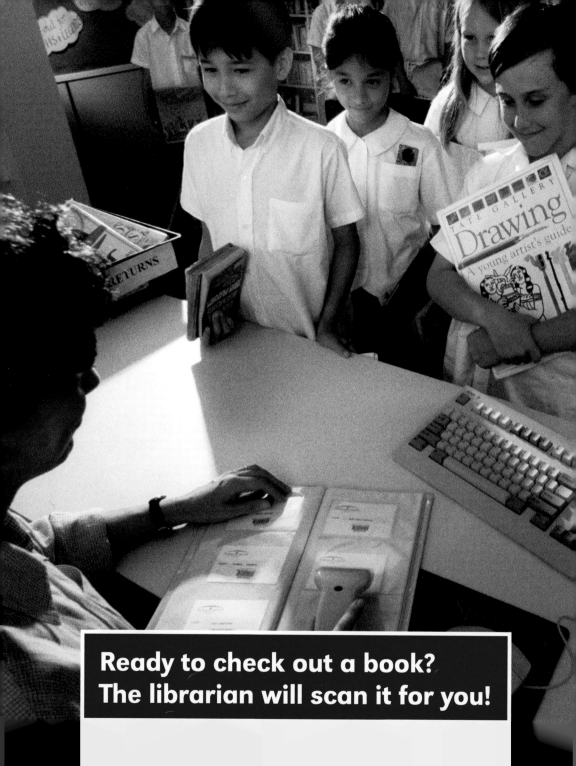

**Ready to check out a book?
The librarian will scan it for you!**

It's **story hour**!

The librarian will read all kinds of books.

Some books may be about animals or faraway places. Other books may be about your favorite characters.

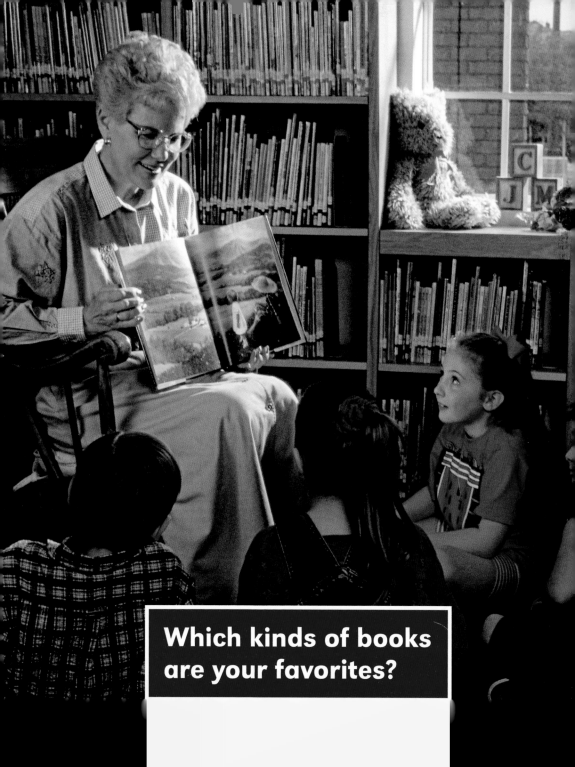

Which kinds of books are your favorites?

Have you ever seen books about the same topic set up on a library table? This is called a **display**.

Librarians make displays about many topics, including holidays and famous people.

Do you like Dr. Seuss? This display features different books he wrote.

The library is a wonderful place. It is a quiet spot where you can learn new things and spend time reading.

Where else can you rent a DVD, use a computer, and find your next favorite book all in one spot?

DO YOU HAVE A LIBRARY CARD?

What will you check out at the library today?

Library Card

CD

Books

Magazines

DVD

YOUR NEW WORDS

call number (**kawl nuhm**-bur) the number that is found on most library items

computer (kuhm-**pyoo**-tur) an electronic machine that can organize information in many ways

display (diss-**play**) a showing of something

librarian (lye-**brer**-ee-uhn) a person who works in a library

library card (**lye**-brer-ee **card**) a card that allows people to borrow items from a library

scanner (**skan**-uhr) a tool that is used to check items out of a library

story hour (**stor**-ee **our**) the time when books are read aloud to children at the library

WHAT ELSE WILL YOU SEE AT A LIBRARY?

book cart

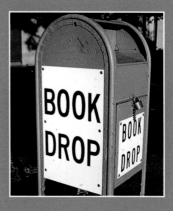

book drop

bookshelves

reading chair

23

INDEX

FIND OUT MORE

Book:

Hoena, B.A. *A Visit to the Library*. Mankato, Minnesota: Capstone Press, 2004.

Website:

Kids' Page: Seminole Public Library
http://www.seminolecountyfl.gov/lls/library/kids/

MEET THE AUTHOR:

Alyse Sweeney is a freelance writer who has published more than twenty books and poems for children. Prior to becoming a freelance writer, she was a teacher, reading specialist, and Scholastic editor. Alyse lives in Las Vegas, Nevada, with her husband and two children.

ML

4/07